BIG AIR
SKATEBOARDING

BY JACK DAVID

BELLWETHER MEDIA • MINNEAPOLIS, MN

Are you ready to take it to the extreme? Torque books thrust you into the action-packed world of sports, vehicles, and adventure. These books may include dirt, smoke, fire, and dangerous stunts. WARNING: read at your own risk.

This edition first published in 2008 by Bellwether Media.

No part of this publication may be reproduced in whole or in part without written permission of the publisher. For information regarding permission, write to Bellwether Media Inc., Attention: Permissions Department, Post Office Box 1C, Minnetonka, MN 55345-9998.

Library of Congress Cataloging-in-Publication Data
David, Jack, 1968-
 Big air skateboarding / by Jack David.
    p. cm. -- (Torque. Action sports)
 Summary: "Photographs of amazing feats accompany engaging information about big air skateboarding. The combination of high-interest subject matter and light text is intended to engage readers in grades 3 through 7"--Provided by publisher.
 Includes bibliographical references and index.
 ISBN-13: 978-1-60014-121-8 (hardcover : alk. paper)
 ISBN-10: 1-60014-121-8 (hardcover : alk. paper)
 1. Skateboarding--Juvenile literature. I. Title.

GV859.8.D37 2008
796.22--dc22   2007016791

CONTENTS

CATCHING AIR

Thousands of fans scream as a skateboarder starts the long roll down the 80-foot **megaramp**. He is traveling between 30 and 40 miles (48.2 and 64.3 kilometers) per hour when he hits the jump. He soars high into the air.

The skateboarder holds his board and does a backflip. He raises his arms as the wheels touch down on the landing ramp. The crowd goes wild. They have just seen a man do a backflip over a 70-foot gap!

FAST FACT

The megaramp is as long as a football field.

WHAT IS BIG AIR SKATEBOARDING?

Big air skateboarding is one of the newest and most thrilling events in skateboarding. Professional skateboarder Danny Way invented the extreme sport in 2004. He has since increased its popularity with events in the U.S., Mexico, and China.

The idea behind big air skateboarding is simple. Competitors drop down a tall entry ramp. They gain speed and sail across a wide gap. While in the air they do flips, spins, and grabs. Then they try to land on the other side before speeding into a 27-foot quarterpipe.

Danny Way

FAST FACT

In 2005, Danny Way became the first man to jump the Great Wall of China on a skateboard.

EQUIPMENT

The biggest piece of big air skateboarding equipment is the megaramp. The huge entry ramp offers skaters two drop-in points. Skaters can choose a drop-in of either 60 or 80 feet (18.3 or 24.4 meters). The gap between the entry ramp and the landing ramp is either 50 or 70 feet (15.2 or 21.3 meters).

Skateboarders need a variety of gear to compete. They need skateboards with strong **trucks**. The trucks connect the wheels to the **deck**. Big air skateboarders also need lots of safety gear. Skateboarders wear helmets, elbow and knee pads, gloves, and padded motorcycle shorts. Shoes and pads need to be taped on so they don't fall off during a high-speed fall.

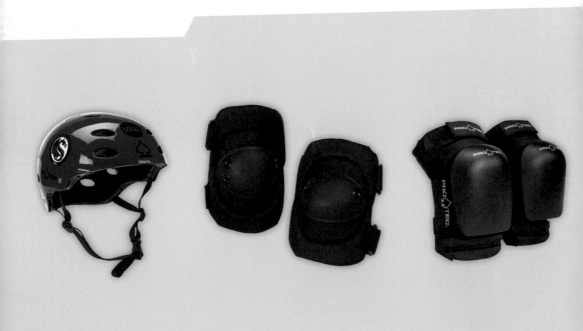

Scoring in big air skateboarding is based on the amount of air a skater gets, the quality and difficulty of the tricks, and the landing. Scoring is based on a 100-point scale. Fifty points come from the initial jump and 50 come from the quarterpipe.

Skaters have four attempts in the **selection session**. The top three skaters from the selection session join the top three finishers from last year in the finals. Each skater now has five attempts to pull off their best trick. Whoever receives the highest single score wins the event that year.

fast fact

Big air skateboarding became an event at the X Games in 2004. Danny Way has won the event in 2004, 2005, and 2006.

Only a small group of elite skaters currently skate big air. This will change as the thrilling extreme sport becomes more common and more skaters build up the courage to attempt the megaramp.

Danny Way stands with son Tavin, Pierre-Luc Gagnon, and Andy Macdonald after winning X Games 11.

GLOSSARY

deck—the surface of a skateboard upon which the skater stands

megaramp—the structure in big air skateboarding; it includes the drop-in, the jump, the landing ramp, and the quarterpipe.

selection session—the first round of a competition which determines who moves on to the finals

truck—the part of a skateboard that connects the wheels to the deck

TO LEARN MORE

AT THE LIBRARY

Doeden, Matt. *Skateboarding*. Mankato, Minn.: Capstone Press, 2005.

Hocking, Justin. *Skateboarding Tricks and Techniques*. New York: PowerKids Press, 2006.

Miller, Connie Colwell. *Skateboarding Big Air*. Mankato, Minn.: Capstone Press, 2007.

ON THE WEB

Learning more about big air skateboarding is as easy as 1, 2, 3.

1. Go to www.factsurfer.com
2. Enter "big air skateboarding" into search box.
3. Click the "Surf" button and you will see a list of related web sites.

With factsurfer.com, finding more information is just a click away.

INDEX